Haunted Inns of Devon

Robert Hesketh

Bossiney Books

Author's acknowledgements

This book was made possible by the active co-operation of the landlords, landladies and inn staff who shared their supernatural experiences with me and who were so helpful in showing me their haunted inns and facilitating the photographs. I offer my thanks to all of them, and also to Torbay Investigators of the Paranormal.

Finally, my thanks to my wife, Adrienne, who accompanied me on my investigations and ably assisted with interviewing and with her own insights into the unseen worlds around us.

Reprinted 2017
First published 2015
by Bossiney Books Ltd, 33 Queens Drive, Ilkley, LS29 9QW
www.bossineybooks.com
© 2015 Robert Hesketh   All rights reserved
ISBN 978-1-906474-51-5

All photographs are by the author. The cover photo shows the Oxenham Arms at south Zeal. The photo on the title page was taken in the Old Church House Inn, Torbryan.

Printed in Great Britain by R Booth Ltd, Penryn, Cornwall

Churston Court at night

Churston Court

'As soon as we arrived at Churston Court Inn a lady on the staff told us of how a shiver went through her as she was stoking the fire in the Armoury Room,' said David Phillips of Torbay Investigators of the Paranormal (TIP). 'She turned to see the tail end of a monk's habit disappearing through the doorway. He's been seen on several occasions. Once a couple saw him pass by one of the bar windows.'

The inn has been the regular meeting place of TIP since 1995 and is said to be on a ley line. Dating from the mid or late 16th century on a settlement site that may well be older, Churston Court has a layered history which may be reflected in the variety of supernatural events TIP has recorded there.

These include sightings of a mother in antique dress, seen in the kitchen with a child hiding behind her skirts. A man in country clothing of a bygone period has also been reported,

Coombe Cellars, Combeinteignhead

as has a woman carrying a heavy book, perhaps the Bible, who passed a guest in the corridor and disappeared through a wall.

TIP have held all night vigils at Churston Court, which included filming and photography. As in several other haunted inns, including the Old Inn Widecombe (page 25) and the Highwayman at Sourton (page 15) orbs of light were captured.

'The question is what are they?' continued David. 'We've captured them on camera in quite a few places. Possibly they're the start of an apparition. With a still photograph they might be reflections caused by a combination of camera flash and dust or water droplets, but when they are captured on camcorders as moving orbs you have something more interesting…'

Another inexplicable phenomenon occurred at TIP's midsummer meeting in 1999.

'We planned an all-night vigil at Berry Pomeroy castle, but first met at Churston Court's Blue Room, where we were surprised to hear a little bell ringing. As far as we knew there was no one else in this part of the building, but we carried on talking. It rang again. Whilst we were trying to work out what it was, it rang a third time right behind our seats. I got up to see whether someone was messing around, but as I stood up there was an almighty bang as though someone had whacked the big oak table we sat at with a huge piece of wood… Two years later, a woman staying in the room above also heard a bell. When she came down to investigate she heard a great bang, just as we had.'

Coombe Cellars, Combeinteignhead

'I've worked for three years at the Coombe Cellars,' said waitress Amber Sadler-Price. 'There were a number of little incidents, such as lights being inexplicably turned on and off, which you could put down to the electrics and this being an old building.

'We know that there was a woman murdered upstairs at the Coombe Cellars long ago. All the girls here used to call her

An interior view at Coombe Cellars

Emma, I don't know why. I've pictured her in my mind, though I don't know where I got the image from. I see her as blonde, with a long blue dress and a pearl necklace, or necklaces, and jewellery.

'The staff often gathered after work in the bar to talk about unexplained manifestations and especially about the murdered woman. It was said she was strangled by a man.

'It was after we started talking about her that I started feeling things,' continued Amber. 'My boyfriend, Dave, said it was all in my head, it wasn't real, but then something happened which changed his mind.

'One night in 2013, when there was no one else here at the Coombe Cellars but us, we were woken by the loudest female scream from the corridor. He thought someone had got in and was playing a trick on us, but when we checked the corridor there was nobody there. That same night a door slammed, but

Cowick Barton Inn

we'd left no doors or windows open to make a draught, though I had a sensation of cold that wasn't physical.

'In the morning, my boyfriend had a shower. Again, we hadn't left any windows or doors open, but the curtains moved, not gently as with a draught, but violently as though someone had hit them.

'After that, I always had a feeling that there was someone there in the corner of our room. I stayed there by myself once. I couldn't take my eyes off that corner, nor sleep. There is definitely, definitely the presence of a female ghost. It was a scary feeling, but I never felt threatened by it. In my head, I felt safe because I'm female, but I sensed she doesn't like men, that she has a vendetta against men as a man killed her.

'My boyfriend had a similar experience when he was here on his own. He felt a sensation of something black over him and a presence pressing down on the bed so that he couldn't move.

'One of the other girls won't stay here alone. If there's no one else staying overnight, she goes to her mum's. When you think of the long history of the Coombe Cellars and how you're tucked away here by yourself it's very spooky. You hear all sorts of strange noises at night…'

Cowick Barton Inn, Exeter

Landlord Lee Squires and his wife Maria had only been at the Cowick Barton Inn for three months when interviewed in 2014, but they had already some direct experience of its supernatural phenomena. These manifestations span several centuries, hardly surprising in view of the inn's long history: it dates from 1540, but had an earlier connection with Cowick Priory.

'The day we first viewed the inn the owner was in Wales and there was no one here, so we showed ourselves around,' said Lee. 'After we'd explored the inn itself, we looked back at it from the garden. I noticed a lady with shoulder length red hair and a white dress watching us from the attic window. Naturally, I thought she must be the owner after all.

'A few weeks later, I met the owner and found she didn't have red hair and she confirmed she had been in Wales when we'd viewed the place. Local customers later told me the red haired woman had been seen five or six times previously.

'Early one morning, I went into the beer cellar to move some barrels,' Lee continued. 'When I returned to the restaurant I could hear someone moving barrels about, but I knew my wife was upstairs and there was no one else in the building. So, I returned to the cellar and found that the barrel which had been standing on top of the others was on the floor. I had to push it aside to open the door.'

Locks have also been mysteriously turned at the Cowick Barton. Lee and his chef found the cubicle door in the men's room locked on the inside. They eventually managed to open the door, but found no one. Maria had a similar experience when she found her bathroom door locked. Gaining no response when she asked to come in, she had to pick the lock. Again, there was nobody there.

Other inexplicable phenomena include a wall-mounted clock which fell from its position, but landed some seven feet away across the bar as if thrown by an unseen hand. Wine glasses too have come crashing from their shelves to land some distance away.

'We've had some very bizarre goings-on. Investigators have had an all-night vigil here and captured moving lights in the attic on their cameras.

'A man who's into the spirit world told me there's the ghost of a large lady here who stands by the main door greeting people and waving them goodbye. His feeling is that she belongs to around 1908. He also told me there's a gentleman from a much earlier period who stands by the fireplace in the Priory Room toasting bread on a fork.

'I haven't seen him myself, but people tell me of a monk who walks across the parking area in front of the inn dragging a body. The story goes that he was making cheese when he heard

The fireplace at Cowick Barton where a ghost toasts his bread

screams and saw his sister being attacked by a man. In defending her, he garrotted her attacker with the cheese wire and cut his head off.'

Devil's Stone Inn, Shebbear

'It was just like putting my hands in a refrigerator,' recalled landlady Chris Hurst, describing her encounter with the ghost of a small girl who haunts the upper landing and bedrooms. 'People hear her light footsteps and laughter as she knocks on doors,' continued Chris. 'They say she's very happy – I hope so.'

Several mediums have visited the 17th century Devil's Stone Inn and agree the girl died in a fire that severely damaged the building. She often announces herself by tugging at people's clothes. 'The fire may have been in 1678,' added Joan Curtis, who knows the Devil's Stone Inn well, having worked there thirty years. 'That's the year on the date stone over the door. When

The bar of the Devil's Stone Inn, Shebbear

the restaurant was renovated the timbers were all found to be charred.

'Different people have had different experiences here. I've always felt at my ease, but several have described the feeling of being watched, especially in the passage… One landlady was on her own, washing her hands at night. The room was lit by a single source and cast her shadow on the wall. She looked up to see another shadow looming over her and growing bigger. She shut her eyes and ran.

'We've had guests who've put a crucifix on the breakfast table to ward off spirits and others who say the room above us is full of laughing children. For some bizarre reason people who sit on the bed in another bedroom always end up crying. Some have seen a friendly man in a red coat and tricorn hat, others a chimney sweep who was a regular customer and died here in 1994 – I

Opposite: The 'Devil's Stone' after which the inn is named

remember him. So you see, ghosts are not always old.'

Before leaving Shebbear we visited the Devil's Stone, from which the pub took its possibly unique name in the 1960s – previously it had been the New Inn. The one tonne stone is unlike other rocks in the area and thought to be a glacial erratic, possibly deposited at the end of the last Ice Age. It stands on the village green by an ancient oak, said to have been a hanging tree. Every November 5th, a team of bellringers armed with stout levers turn it to keep the village safe from disaster for another year by crushing the power of Satan and proclaiming the triumph of good over evil.

Golden Fleece, Holsworthy

'We've found a mummified cat in the roof and an old leather shoe, both of which were placed there to ward off witchcraft,' explained landlord Bruce Priddy, who takes a great interest in the Golden Fleece's long and varied history going back to medieval times when it was a thatched farmhouse.

'I'm a natural born sceptic, but there've been some very weird happenings. One day my step-father found all the furniture in the bar had been turned upside down overnight. Another time, the door leading to the stairs banged loudly and repeatedly late one evening. This brought me downstairs in a flurry, only to find my mother in the bar doing the crossword and looking equally perplexed.

'Once, we had a young lady staying with us. She was very distressed, having just split up with her boyfriend. One day, she came down to breakfast to thank my mother for talking so kindly to her last evening. My mother was surprised and said she hadn't spoken to the lady and had been fast asleep at the time.

'"So, what happened?' asked my mother.

'"Well, this lady who looked like you in a black Victorian dress

The Golden Fleece, Holsworthy

spoke to me when I was lying in bed. She said: 'Don't worry, everything will be fine. Time will be a healer; you just have to trust. You'll get back together with your boyfriend and marry him.'" This duly happened – they're still happily married with children and live locally.

'My mother was not surprised at this encounter, as she had seen the lady in black several times and found her very kind and thoughtful, the sort of person who can't bear to see people upset. She appeared again on other occasions to comfort people.

'Some dogs are very sensitive,' continued Bruce. 'We had one that would growl at the chair by the long case clock every time he passed it as though there was someone sitting in it. This went on for several weeks. We asked a local chap called Frank Ward, the "Singing Coalman of Holsworthy", who was very sensitive to the supernatural, to contact whatever spirit it was who sat in the chair.

'Frank did this one day after the pub was shut. We watched him talking and nodding his head at the chair. Then he said: "That's all done, he won't appear again. He was a farmer who died of a long-standing lung complaint. He wanted desperately to get in contact with someone in the house who was suffering from lung complaints and tell them to look after themselves properly." I realised this was aimed at my mother, who suffered from lung infections all her life and eventually died from lung disease.'

The Highwayman, Sourton

One of the most haunted areas of the unique Highwayman Inn is the Rita Jones Locker Bar, which includes fittings from the tragic 19th century whaling ship *Diana*. Disaster overtook *Diana* in the winter of 1866-67, when she became trapped in Arctic pack ice. 'We will not have a moment's peace of mind or body so long as we are in this awful ice,' one crewman wrote in his log. Twelve men and the captain succumbed to scurvy before the survivors forced the ship back to Grimsby with their bodies.

The Rita Jones Locker Bar at The Highwayman

It seems the trauma of that terrible voyage is imprinted on the *Diana's* very timbers. Many guests have remarked on the strange atmosphere of the bar and its sense of cold. Landlady Sally Thomson authorised a night-time séance and was astounded by what she saw radiating from the door of the old whaling ship.

'They weren't physical forms, but orbs of light, which is the closest I've ever come to seeing the supernatural,' said Sally. 'I went to bed that night almost not believing what I'd seen, and then waking the next morning to realize I'd indeed seen something extraordinary.

'Guests often report they see or feel things here at the Highwayman,' she continued. 'Some ask if they can conduct night vigils, but I don't allow them, preferring to deal with two people I know and trust.

'I'd love to tell you all sorts of tales of hauntings, and perhaps I should from a business point of view, but I'll just tell you what

The Hideaway Bar at The Highwayman

I know. My mum, Rita – the bar we've just been in was named in her honour – was very tuned in to spiritual things and saw the figure of a Cavalier with a feather in his hat passing through the bar and on through the wall. He appeared repeatedly at ten in the morning, which is peculiar. We associate him with the Civil War Battle of Sourton Down in 1643. As Sourton was Roundhead, I suspect there was a woman involved – that usually makes men act out of character.'

Mysterious footsteps have also been heard at the Highwayman, notably by the Ghost Research Foundation in 2002. Pausing from their investigations to take breakfast in the Rita Jones Bar, they were startled by the sound of heavy boots tramping the deserted floor above. Abandoning their food, they rushed upstairs with their cameras hoping to record the phenomena. When the films were developed a 'vortex', a swirl of light, was clearly discernible in an otherwise deserted corridor.

People staying overnight at the Highwayman have been mysteriously locked in or out of the Victorian Bedroom. One guest reported her shoes had been moved, another that cushions in the room had been flattened as though someone had sat on them whilst she was out. Her husband photographed the room and was convinced the resulting digital images showed a foggy moving figure.

Have Sally or her husband, Bruce, been disturbed by similar manifestations?

'I've lived here at the Highwayman nearly all my life and never feel uncomfortable,' said Sally. 'I tell guests about the hauntings if they're interested, but I don't if they're not because it's a horrible experience to stay in a place if you're frightened. I think sometimes the boyfriends and husbands exaggerate things so their ladies will cuddle up to them and feel protected!'

Kingsbridge Inn, Totnes

'I'd heard the place was haunted, but I was sceptical at first,' said Alex Young, landlord of the 17th century Kingsbridge Inn, Totnes, where supernatural phenomena have been reported over many years. 'There was a lot of work to do when my brother and I took over in 2011, but tools and other things kept going missing. This was odd, but it was much stranger when I tried to take photographs of our work. There was no problem photographing the bar, but my digital camera just went blank when I tried to photograph the restaurant. At this point I felt freezing cold.'

The restaurant is where the body of Mary Brown is said to be walled up. She was a barmaid at the inn and was made pregnant by the then landlord, a married man. He is said to have murdered her and hidden her body to keep the disgraceful affair secret.

Alex experienced other inexplicable phenomena, especially in the restaurant...

'Lights would stay on, even when switched off. Glasses would crash off a table and candles shoot from their fittings. On our opening night, the kitchen was barricaded with a chair. This happened again several times afterwards.

'At first, I thought we were haunted only by Mary's ghost, but now I've had the place investigated by paranormal groups and mediums I'm sure there are other spirits.'

After the customers had left at the end of one evening, Alex and his assistant Ruth joined mediums in the restaurant. Although the heating was on, Alex had an intense sensation of cold when the mediums claimed to contact Mary. Some weeks later, the mediums returned with their voice recordings of the séance.

'We couldn't hear a lot, but there was a distinct gasp from a woman – Mary, I guess. Then there was a really aggressive man, saying something which I couldn't make out, but it sounded nasty. Then there was another silence and a gasp, and then it sounded as though Mary was telling us to go, go, go as though she was getting really upset. The whole experience was bizarre, a real eye opener…'

Although the restaurant area appears to be the centre of supernatural activity, the mediums believe other spirits are active in the upstairs apartment and also in the function room at the back of the inn. They told Alex that someone had met a violent death there by falling from a height.

Old Church House Inn, Torbryan

'There's a presence throughout the building,' said Kane Clarke, landlord at the medieval Old Church House Inn. 'Long ago, when I first came to the inn as a student, I put my experiences down to having too many pints at the bar. But now I don't drink on the job and I still experience things.

'Little things happen every day. Disembodied footsteps are commonplace, especially in the roof void above bedroom 12. Objects appear and disappear… Many visitors have seen orbs of light; my wife sees them too, but I see people as clearly as I see you.

Inside the Old Church House Inn at Torbryan

'I see groups of people in period dress, mainly Victorian. The first time I saw them I was really startled and leapt out of bed, but now I'm quite blasé, say "hello" and go back to sleep.

'In the early days here, I saw a little girl running around the bar one evening. Naturally, I thought it was my small daughter and told her to get back to bed. I went to check upstairs and found her fast asleep.

'Where we are in the lounge there's the distinct smell of a lady's perfume. Usually, it's the perfume I sense and very strongly. On the rare occasions I've seen the lady, she's in Victorian dress with a bustle.

'Above us is a coffin hatch, a trap door in the ceiling used to lower heavy objects – including bodies that were too big for the narrow stairs – down from the room above. The stairs have long gone, but people (including me) have seen disembodied feet and legs descending from the floor above.'

Kane led us through to the bar, where the wooden panelling is thought to be recycled ship's timber and to date from the time of the Spanish Armada. The side facing the bar was probably for the officers' mess as it is finely finished, whilst the opposite side may have been for the crew's mess as it is rougher. Some people have seen faces emerging from the panels on the officers' side, where keys were hung from hooks and, with the rocking of the ship, have worn distinct arcs in the wood.

Musical evenings are held in the bar and are even more popular than they appear to be. People who've taken photographs of them have been surprised to find faces in the audience who weren't there – at least in the physical sense. Kane believes it is the music that attracts them.

Some living guests have come specifically to meet the inn's apparitions. However, it seems these don't necessarily come when bidden, but may arrive unexpectedly. One curious couple had resigned themselves to experiencing nothing out of the ordinary after staying several times in different rooms. The husband's scepticism was strengthened, though the wife remained a believer in the supernatural. On their last visit he woke up in the middle of the night with the impression that something or someone was sitting on his legs. He felt paralysed and couldn't rise or even turn to wake up his wife…

The inn's haunted reputation attracted the attention of the producers of *Most Haunted*, a TV programme investigating the paranormal. Kane refused their requests to visit at first, as filming would disrupt business, but eventually relented on condition the crew didn't antagonise the presences at the inn. At the time of writing (2014), the film could be seen on You Tube. It includes a considerable number of alleged supernatural experiences.

Kane had a further incident to add, relating to a set of old handmade nails he keeps behind the bar as a souvenir of the crew's stay. Visiting the adjoining cottages, one of the crew had casually asked that any presence make itself known. The nails promptly landed at his feet, one after the other.

'I've hosted psychic weekends here,' continued Kane, 'but only when everyone involved is like-minded. Equally, we've had a local paranormal investigation group and some mediums stay. One medium made me smile when she told me the inn's ghosts like me because I'm polite to them and bid them goodnight.

'Only two or three times have I felt uncomfortable, but I put that down to the dark and the way the wind howls down the chimney. I don't believe there's anything malicious or harmful at the inn. These are presences that want to be here. People who've experienced things at the Old Church House talk of having a warm, a welcoming, healing feeling.

'You don't really own a lovely ancient building like this; it owns you, it envelops your whole life. Although the inn requires constant repairs, I've become very fond of it. We've been here ten years, but are just custodians: the Old Church House will be here for hundreds of years after we're gone. Other landlords and ladies will come and go. When our time's up, we'll pass it on to another custodian of its history. All that we can ask is that the time we're here will be remembered well.'

The Old Inn, Widecombe

'Usually, Harry appears quite solid and normal and later fades away into nothing,' explained Assistant Manager James Houghton in describing The Old Inn's resident spirit, who has been reported by a number of guests over many years. 'We've had several different descriptions of him, but all agree he wears a black hat and old fashioned clothes. He's been seen in older areas of the inn, but never in the new parts. Most often, he appears in winter, maybe because the inn's much quieter then – it's sometimes so busy in summer he might not be noticed!'

Harry was most recently seen in 2013, by a guest at the 14th

According to 'Widecombe Fair', Devon's best known folk song, the ghost of Tom Pearce's Old Grey Mare (who died carrying Uncle Tom Cobley and all to Widecombe Fair) haunts the surrounding moor:

> *When the wind whistles cold on the moor of a night,*
> *All along, down along, out along lee;*
> *Tom Pearce's old mare doth appear ghostly white…'*

century inn. She first noticed him standing near her by the fire-side in the bar.

'This lady was quite matter of fact,' continued James. 'She told me she is sensitive to the supernatural, whereas I don't think I am. At least, I've never seen him and I lived upstairs here for fifteen years, but I have seen things going on which I think he's been doing.

'Before we moved the bar to its present position we had glasses hanging from the ceiling in the middle room and they'd swing on their hooks. One would swing at one end of the line,

Inside the Old Inn, Widecombe

another at the other end. If you let them alone, then that would be it, but if you stopped them yourself, two others would start to go. Another one would rock and then he'd start knocking more and before you knew it you'd have all of them swinging and then they'd start to get a little more violent…'

James described how one of the heavy pewter tankards suddenly shot off the shelf above the fireplace in the middle bar and landed in the centre of the room. Perhaps Harry or some other spirit or spirits were behind this and a perplexing event in the kitchen too.

'When we came down one morning the chef said to me: 'You must have had a drink or two last night.' I said I hadn't, but he asked me to have a look at the kitchen, where a ball of string we'd left there was woven in around the kitchen equipment.'

The *Myths and Legends* team from BBC2 filmed at the Old Inn and failed to record anything out of the ordinary. However, two amateur ghost hunters claimed to have had more success in 2011 when they recorded inexplicable orbs of light in the middle room around the fireplace.

'They had what looked like an ordinary digital camera and showed me the exposures they'd just taken,' said James. 'Being the sceptic that I am, I thought what they showed me was perhaps a reflection – but no, it was something special and I was impressed. As far as I know they did nothing to the digital image and wouldn't have had time to manipulate it.'

Some might say so much paranormal activity would warrant further investigation. James, though, is adamant this is not wanted at the Old Inn: 'We haven't had any séances here. I wouldn't want to upset Harry. True, he throws things about a bit, but he's never hurt or frightened anybody. He seems an amiable chap. He and I have got on well for years! I leave him alone and he leaves me alone.'

Oxenham Arms, South Zeal

'We have several spiritual residents, people who've lived here in the past and make their presence known from time to time,' said Simon Powell, who, with his wife Lyn, bought the Oxenham Arms in 2012. 'Perhaps because of the history of the Oxenham Arms – it dates back to medieval times – all these manifestations are pleasant. There's nothing frightening here. It's rather that other folk are ingrained in the fabric of the building.

'Mary Oxenham, who lived in the late 16th century, is the one most often seen. Different people describe her in the same way. She's quite short, in her thirties and wears a long white dress. A monk frequents the passage and a former landlord has also been seen, smoking his pipe by the bar fire as he did in life.'

Simon and Lyn felt strongly drawn to the Oxenham Arms as soon as they saw it. However, the inn had then been closed for nearly a year and needed a deal of restoration to bring it to its present high standard. The Powells received help from an unexpected quarter shortly after their arrival.

'The electricity was off and everything was covered in mould and dust. Lyn said she wished she'd had the opportunity to clean up properly before her sister came to see it… Well, we locked up at the end of our first day with the one and only set of keys and returned these to the estate agent in Okehampton, as we were required to do as the inn wasn't yet ours in law.

'Early next day, we collected the keys and returned with the electrician. To our amazement, everything – the till, the bar, the floor – had been meticulously cleaned, to the extent that every glass had been wiped, as well as all the optics, which you have to remove to clean. A glass of red wine on the bar had been carefully wiped too – but the contents left. Someone must've come in here during the night and done a thorough job without electric light. As the estate agents had changed the main locks and the former landlord confirmed there was only one set of keys, the whole affair remains a mystery.'

An exceptional, if not unique feature of the Oxenham Arms is the enormous granite menhir, a prehistoric standing stone, that is part of the building's fabric and predates it by some 4000 years. It is thought to be well over twenty feet long, with half of it beneath ground and Simon hopes a geophysical survey will reveal more about its full extent and what might lie beneath it.

Visitors can see it in the room behind the bar, where it stands proud from the wall. It also extends into the Bovey Room on the floor above, where several strange phenomena have occurred.

'When we were renovating the inn, I stayed in the Bovey Room,' continued Simon. 'Every night at half past two I was woken by someone calling my name. This happened six or seven times.

'You never know for sure whether you're dreaming these things or not, so I set my alarm for quarter past two. I waited… and about a quarter to three I heard a lady's voice shout my name. I thought it might be someone having a joke, so I checked

26

The Oxenham Arms by night (above) and the bar (below)

around the building, but all the lights were off and no one was there.

'James, a builder friend of ours, had a strange experience staying in the same room on his own. One morning when we met him for breakfast, he wasn't talking to us at all. When we chaffed him about it, he said he was OK, but something strange had happened to him during the night. At about two in the morning, he was convinced someone, a lady, had climbed into bed with him… It wasn't a piece of wishful thinking, I'm sure – James never jokes about anything! Moreover, there was no one else staying here at the time. Anyway, he refused to sleep there again.

'After we'd opened, two guests said they'd been woken in the night by someone stroking them on the arm,' added Lyn. 'It wasn't frightening; they found it strangely comforting, a really nice, warm feeling. Another guest reported lights appearing under the floor, but we have no under-floor lighting.'

Although they had no experience of the supernatural before taking over the Oxenham Arms, Simon and Lyn are unperturbed by its inexplicable phenomena.

'Whilst we own the Oxenham Arms, we very much believe we're really only caretakers, part of its long history,' said Simon. 'Sitting on our own here on a quiet evening, we feel surrounded by love and warmth.'

The Three Crowns, Chagford

'I was cleaning in the bedroom suite one afternoon,' said Amanda Moreton, talking of the first time she worked at The Three Crowns as a sixteen year old in 1983. 'I turned around and watched Mary Whiddon walk straight through the wall. She was very young, still in her teens I would say, both frail and angelic. Although it wasn't my first experience of seeing a ghost, I was really shocked and just ran out of the room screaming my head off. When the landlady asked another chambermaid to take over, she said casually, "Oh, we see Mary all the time."'

The Three Crowns at Chagford

Amanda already knew the history of The Three Crowns, which originated as the Whiddon's family home. She also knew of Mary Whiddon's tragic death here after she was shot and fatally wounded on her wedding day in 1641 by a jealous former lover at St Michael's church opposite.

'A couple who stayed overnight said they needed to speak to me,' continued Amanda. 'They told me they were spiritualists and a child had followed them to bed with the message that I must tell the true story of Mary Whiddon.

'As I understand it, Mary really was in love with the first man, her murderer. However, her family needed money to save their family home – what later became the Three Crowns. They were offered a dowry for Mary to marry a much older man, a friend of her father's, so that's why she jilted her first love, and he shot her in rage.'

Amanda returned to the Three Crowns as receptionist in

The ghost William Whiddon's armchair at the Three Crowns. He can get quite indignant if the fire is not lit for him.

2012. She soon encountered Mary again:

'I was on my own typing at the reception desk one evening and suddenly had the feeling that someone was watching me. I turned to find a lady standing by the coffee machine. She didn't look quite as I remembered her from all those years ago, but she was still very young. She wore a buff calico dress and her hair was in braids. Although she just stood there watching me, I wasn't freaked out this time, she didn't scare or threaten me at all. As she approached me she suddenly disappeared and I haven't seen her since, though I would like to.

'I'm not the only person who's seen Mary. A guest said she saw her leaning against a pillar in the bar sobbing, whilst a young lad, just seventeen, who worked here as night porter, actually left because of Mary. One night he was cleaning the shelves when he suddenly felt uncomfortable. He straightened up to find Mary

on the other side of the bar. He ran out of the building screaming and phoned the police with his story. Of course, they just
laughed at him. Reluctantly, he came back, but later saw Mary
on the office CCTV. After that he left, he simply couldn't cope.'

Amanda has never seen the spirit of Sir Sidney Godolphin, a
Royalist officer who was fatally wounded in 1643, when Royalists
attacked Chagford, which inclined to Parliament. Godolphin
and his men attempted to storm The Three Crowns, then
Wyddon House, where the Roundhead commander, Northcote,
and his officers were billeted. Seriously wounded in the thigh,
Godolphin's loss of blood was so severe that he died in the porch
of the inn. Meanwhile, his men forced an entry, but Northcote's
party escaped by scrambling out of the back.

'The builders who renovated The Three Crowns in 2012
refused to sleep here because they were convinced they could
hear Godolphin marching along the corridors at night. I must
admit the hairs on the back of my neck stand on end when I
walk the corridor by one particular room. The feeling I get on
that corridor is bad, but it's not Mary, I am sure.

'There is also talk of a third spirit, William Whiddon, who
sits in an armchair beside the fire in the bar. He was mayor and
magistrate at Chagford. Those accused of crimes were brought
before Whiddon at the inn. He was very annoyed indeed when
the fire wasn't lit for him during the recent renovation work, but
he should be happier now it's burning regularly.'

Valiant Soldier, Buckfastleigh

Visiting the Valiant Soldier gives a strong impression of stepping
back into the past. It dates from at least 1747 and is known as
'the pub where "time" was never called'.

When it closed in 1965, licensees Mark and Alice Roberts,
who had been there since 1939, lived on as recluses, hoarding
the everyday objects of their lives and keeping the pub exactly
as it was – even down to the change left in the till. Much later, it
was opened to the public as a fascinating piece of recent social

history, along with the adjoining museum and tourist information centre.

'Many visitors and some of our volunteer guides have told me of their unease and inexplicable feelings of coldness,' said Sandra Coleman, retired manager of the Valiant Soldier. 'Working here certainly felt eerie. This was especially so when I was on my own, as though I was intruding on someone else's space. Those feelings were strongest upstairs in the corridor, bedroom and lounge where the Roberts used to live. Doors would bang, but when I checked them they were open and there was no draught.

'One dark afternoon, when I was working at the desk by the entrance, I saw a young man come down the stairs. Ghosts were the last subject I had on my mind and I was keen to lock up and go home... but I find I encounter strange things when I least expect them.

'Anyway, I asked my colleague to go over and request our visitor to buy a ticket... but when we looked again the young man had vanished. At that time we were opening what's now the museum and archive upstairs and I rather think it was the building work which disturbed this spirit.'

With so much reported supernatural activity, it is not surprising that the museum and the Valiant Soldier have drawn paranormal investigators, including the paranormal investigation team, Haunted Devon. At the upstairs listening point by the archive room, visitors can hear a fascinating verbal account by a medium. She describes her spiritual impressions in various rooms, her most vivid being of a man who, with his small black dog, was a regular visitor at the inn.

Apparently, he was a rather shady character and was involved

Opposite, top: A bedroom at the Valiant Soldier in Buckfastleigh, which is a museum rather than a pub, reflecting the life of the publicans as well as the arrangement of the bar – shown in the lower picture

in a brawl at the inn. Struck down, he hit his head violently upon some hard object and died instantly, forcing him to leave a life he was enjoying. He remains a 'grounded spirit' at the Valiant Soldier.

Warren House Inn, near Postbridge

'I'm sceptical to say the least,' said Peter Parsons, who's been landlord of the remote Warren House Inn on Dartmoor since 1988. 'But sometimes when I go outside on my own at night I know I'm not alone, although I don't feel under any threat.

'It's eerie here, especially once we've switched the generator off at night. There's no mains electricity and no light pollution so it's really dark on cloudy nights. Like any old building, you can hear every creak, every little sound... When I first came here I could hear noises like footsteps at night, but I knew there was no one else anywhere near. All the same, every once in a while something possessed me to go and look...

'There is a story that long ago a guest staying here in the mid-

34

William Toop Stephens

dle of winter opened a chest in his room and discovered the salted corpse of an old man. The landlord told him not to worry as it was only father and they were waiting for better weather and the ground to thaw before burying him.'

However, Peter doesn't think it's the old man who's prowling around. Nor does he believe it's the miner from Vitifer mine opposite who is said to have been killed in a brawl with another miner at the pub in the mid-19th century, but rather it's William Toop Stephens, the landlord who shot himself at the bar in 1929.

Stephens' photograph hangs in the dining area, whilst other photographs show his family and the Warren House Inn in decades past. In a glass cabinet is a newspaper cutting from the *Exeter Gazette* of 26 March 1929, reporting the inquest of his sad death. Mary Annie Stephens, his widow, stated:

> We had no trouble except that my husband had taken more drink of late. He had never threatened to take his life. We never liked to see him handle a gun when he had any drink, it made him obstinate and trouble-some… I searched the house for letters, but found none.

The newspaper report concluded: 'The Coroner returned a verdict that the deceased died from gunshot wounds self-inflicted, whilst in an unsound state of mind.'

The West Country Inn, near Hartland

'Spirits? It's not a question of belief, it's a question of sensitivity,' said Françoise Lechatier, Assistant Manager of the West Country Inn, which has served locals and travellers on the North Devon road to Cornwall for at least three hundred years. 'Some people are more sensitive to atmosphere than others. Me, I can't stand a bad atmosphere, I walk away. Here it is happy, can't you sense it?'

Françoise led my wife Adrienne and myself to the flagstones in front of the dining room fire.

'Many people have reported supernatural activity at this spot, including mediums who visit the inn each winter for the annual ghost hunt.

'I never feel alone. But I'm not scared – why should I be? There are two here, men, one old and one young. It's strange, but not unpleasant. One of them has put his arms around my shoulders

Adrienne, rapt in concentration

and is tickling me... Adrienne, you stand there. What you can sense?

Adrienne stood intently for some time, before saying: 'He knows I'm not you and he's amused. I have a picture of him in my mind. He's quite young with blond hair, but he's not touching because he knows I'm married to Robert!

'He was a farm labourer. The older man enjoying his drink has dark hair and was a regular customer here too. I think he was a jack of all trades. If a job needed doing around here, he did it.

'Ah, he's turned to the other and said, "She's good, isn't she!"

The West Country Inn, beside the A39 near Hartland

They're a jolly pair and interested in me because they know I'm a local too. It's most peculiar, like having a chat with them. I can hear and answer them in my head…'

Meanwhile, I was standing between the two women with my digital voice recorder, but had been unaware throughout this strange episode of anything beyond my five senses. In the pause that followed, I asked Françoise why she thinks these two spirits are grounded at the inn.

'I don't know, there are so many theories. Some say spirits are grounded because they are restless, but these men are not unhappy, so come on! If they have a pain, they do not complain of it. You hear about howling spirits, but you don't howl, do you?' she asked, turning to what appeared to be empty space to me.

'This was a place of safety. They want to stay because they were happy here. I don't know if the inn is a doorway to somewhere else. Maybe this is a sanctuary for them until their minds, their spirits, are ready to journey on.'

We three made the journey upstairs to see the bedrooms. In one there is a recurrent and inexplicable smell of smoke, perhaps dating from a long ago fire which clearly damaged a large part of the inn, particularly this room, scorching the timbers.

In another room, mischief is afoot.

'You turn the lights off when you leave the room,' explained Françoise, 'and you find the TV blaring away when you come back. It happened to me yesterday. I went to get the room key and it wouldn't work. I tried to turn it – and the door is open and the television is off. I know I'm not mad! Then I come back and the lights will be on. I turn them off and come back to find one light is on. I come back again and the other one is on. Playful, yes? When I sleep in that room it takes a while to convince myself everything is fine.'

We moved on to James's room. 'Who is James?' I asked.

'He's the ghost,' continued Françoise matter-of-factly, as she greeted him. 'He was a soldier and likes everything here in order, very demanding. He moves things his own way if he does not like them.'

'Au revoir, James,' she said as we left the room.

The restaurant area of the Kingsbridge Inn, Totnes, which the owners initially found impossible to photograph – see page 17

More about West Country ghosts from Bossiney Books

Ghostly encounters, Peter Underwood
Ghosts around Bodmin Moor, Michael Williams
Ghosts of Cornwall, Peter Underwood
Ghosts of Devon, Peter Underwood
Ghosts of Dorset, Peter Underwood
Ghosts of North Devon, Peter Underwood
Ghosts of Somerset, Peter Underwood
Supernatural Dartmoor, Michael Williams
West Country Hauntings, Peter Underwood